W9-AGZ-601

THE FLAME CHARTS

ALSO BY PAUL OPPENHEIMER

Before a Battle and Other Poems

Beyond the Furies, new poems

Till Eulenspiegel, His Adventures

The Birth of the Modern Mind: Self, Consciousness and the
  Invention of the Sonnet

Evil and the Demonic: A New Theory of Monstrous Behavior

Infinite Desire: A Guide to Modern Guilt

Rubens, A Portrait: Beauty and the Angelic

Blood Memoir, or The First Three Days of Creation (*novel*)

THE FLAME CHARTS

New Poems

Paul Oppenheimer

SPUYTENDUYVIL

© 2002 Paul Oppenheimer
ISBN 1-881471-87-X
cover art © Burt Hasen

Spuyten Duyvil
PO Box 1852
Cathedral Station
NYC 10025
http://spuytenduyvil.net
1-800-886-5304

Acknowledgements

A number of these poems, including the longer ones, first appeared in the journals or with the publishers cited here, and for whose interest in my work I am grateful: "Auras and Haloes: An Investigation of Images" in *Asylum*; "Magma," "City" and "Lines for a Drawing by Burt Hasen" in *Frank: An International Journal of Contemporary Writing and Art*; "Letter from Aiolia" in *The Literary Review*; "The Trek to the Far Corners of the Earth" in *Mencard 108*, The Menard Press (London); "Finding her Photograph," "Into," "Manhattan Psalm" and "Aftermath" in *Poetry in Performance*; "My Antique French Clock" and "After the Empire Fell" in *Tenth Decade* (London); "Still Life: Banana" in *Promethean*; "Seaside" and "Cellini's Flight from Italy" in *Alea 6.*

CONTENTS

Magma	1
City	2
The Hypothesis of Space	5
Manhattan Psalm	7
Post-Modern Catalectic Glyconics	8
Nude Woman	9
Finding her Photograph	10
Aftermath	11
Liquid	12
Color Étude	13
Autumn Specimens	14
Still Life: Banana	15
The Trek to the Far Corners of the Earth	16
Sometimes	17
Orpheus	18
Letter from Aiolia	19
Jonah Awakens to his Mission as Prophet	20
After the Empire Fell	21
Cellini's Flight from Italy	22
Still Life: Crucifixion	28
La Sainte-Chapelle	29
Lines for a Drawing by Burt Hasen	31
Swinburne and Maupassant at Étretat	32
Auras and Haloes: An Investigation of Images	33
The Theory of Soaring	39
Rendezvous	40
My Antique French Clock	41
The Scrollwork Aspects	42
The Training á la Diogenes	43
Moving Picture	44
How the World Began	45
The Blazing Age	47
The Flame Charts	48
Still Life: The Garden of Ptolemy	49
Caladium	50
The Universe of Streets	51
Rushes and Grafts	52
Seaside	53
Into	55

The Flame Charts

MAGMA

The hot flow essential, black with animal heat—
I take it for my poems, this magma
Black with beast heat, deep combustion,
Core-grace, the chant of heart explosion
Thrumming in the planet's chest
Vibrating in the earth-lungs
Aching, beating itself into flames
The esemplastic powerful roar of freedom
Down, down below the earth-crust—
I haul it through my body-mouth,
Ride its hot blowing through lungs and lips,
The primitive essential stammer below,
Above, the universal streaming magma,
The blast mathematical, sexual, amazed at its own freedom
Volcanic, exploding into its shiny frozen form.

CITY

City of apartments blown from the galaxy's core,
City of lights that mimic the core's creative light
Burning there where the blast of intelligence blew,
Blows and keeps blowing down through the telescopes,
A pure white knuckle onto photographic paper,
Brilliant micronic creative spot—
City planned ten billion years ago

City of plane geometry mined from light,
Mathematical city, aflame with sacred numbers, calculations
Worshipped from towers and sewers and intellectual bridges,
Cherished in cannibal visions of luxury by thieves and gods,
Madmen, madwomen, grown filthy with desire,
Grown vulgar with misalliance far from the galaxy's core—
City wholesome with swanky vulgarity

City of surprised grace like a doe glimpsed in a glade,
Sunlit doe-city, with sudden waterfalls and grass
And ways of vanishing and sunny reappearances,
City of multiplying theaters multiplying bright streets,
Anonymous sunlit actors in abandoned parks,
Brilliant music-city, parade-city—
City of murder most foul

I know your terrors and shinings, your nurslings and deaths,
Your corpses made ridiculous with dwarfings like sparrows,
Filth-gray fluff bits, squabbling on fire escapes, jerking,
Sniping, unthinking—I know your quadratic pleasures,
Your architecture obscene and your buildings like egrets,
Elegant, smart, prissy, proven,

Floridian with perpetual youth and electricity and fountains,
I know your tunics of rivers besplattered with industrial stains,
Those rivers barely rinsed before folding into the Atlantic,
Rivers turning from tunics into snakes at their folding,
Surrealist serpents at the Battery
Uncoiling their scales in sunlight,
Brilliant bearers of evil tidings—

I know your magic rivers of commerce and borders,
I know your territorial rivers of tidings,
I rejoice in their cartographic strainings and powers,
Hum with their credential droplets, brutish molecules—
The brashness of an island-country city
Brash in its awakening alleys

I know the obsidian midnight of your Sheep Meadow, its black grass
Unundulating flatness forming a uniform square,
I know this midnight facing towers and towers
And always at my back hear the muted masses whispering in a roll,
The drumming sighs of masses whispering,
Inarticulate breezings of them,
I hear their floppy useless documents,
Perennial questions, rolling—

Behind me, always behind me, facing the towers, their rolling
Forward against my midnight eyes, cherished lightning, rolling
Their cotillion of the Milky Way miniaturized, and
Know the universe as window. Through blank panes
I glimpse the trace of other blanker panes,
The amused huge transparencies of spirit—
The amused spirit-city of the universe!

As the universe rocks back and forth on one jet fulcrum,

The point inside, outside that Archimedes wanted,
The point always waiting, alive, esemplastic, polyplastic,
One central point of rocking perpetual motion,
Great skirts settling—for whatever endlessly rocks must be finite,
Dimensions of light geometrized,
With speed and energy, the equal alleys of reason—

So here this city rocks and settles, making the endless point.
I know your rocking point, your blasts and peace, its Empyrean grace,
Your nervous shining energy, credentialing, marbling, electrifying,

Your always perpetual sources like fresh immigrants from nations, and
From the nation, travelers to the point, pilgrims of planning—
I know how you dream of the sex of angels, rushing downstream,
Giddy with the enthusiasm of beasts,
Angel beasts, chessplayers with your dark—

I know your orchid ecstasies, epiphitic, rootless as the air,
Rootless as your monuments to your potent military dead,
Those flying with oxidization into green changes, grassy graffiti, and
Your tumble of tilting fluids cruising your nerves—
Electrified news of corruption,
Your exquisite steel beauty, and

I see God your great anthropologist, practical magician
Cataloguing your primitive concepts of his commissions,
With the casualness of gravity soaking you up,
Soaking and loosing you in these communities of desire—
Each of you a penthouse, inventory house
Cleansed with the griefs of the ego,
The ego's perpetual griefs,

And blaze with you in your spiritual mathematics.

THE HYPOTHESIS OF SPACE

Fog is also a storm, and like a cyclone an obliterator, a banisher, an opulescent blaster, more precise than thunder or the crash of an August rain that wheels sharply, an emperor's arrogant chariot, across the landscape, twists and vanishes. Fog works with an anesthetist's calm, a cunning awe, a stride like apocalypse, but one that is infinitely subtle, a dissolving as of candy on the tongue, yet always powerful as the arousal-seconds of sex, or the flattery of your woman's smile.

Try it out. Take one of the wooden deck chairs on the South Street Pier at seven o'clock, on a tangy evening in January, below the Brooklyn Bridge, a hot chocolate in hand, coat loosened, the queered air of the fish market in your nostrils, eyes wandering to the lit bridge, and across the river to the bright necklaces of lights on the Brooklyn side. You see the swart muscles of the factory buildings over there, and then red neon spelling Watchtower, white neon below that counting the time, 7:03, platinum bulbs in crisscross rows stenciling a restaurant at the river's edge, and not a boat in sight in between, the river runic without current or outline. Past the bridge, looking upriver, you see the Manhattan Bridge, also alight at its pillars, along its arcs, with its rivers of traffic aglow and bisecting the river turned invisible beneath. As your eyes wander back, the lights on the Manhattan side of the river arch and hump in feline curves away from you, rippling uptown. On the Brooklyn side, similar lights rub the sky in an undulation towards Queens.

The fog moves in, perambulates.

At first you do not notice. As it gathers, opens, you begin to choose in yourself a novel emotion, religious, acute, of plasmic surprise. The surprise comes from detecting absences in yourself, obliterations and allotments, through thin opaque lenses in you, as in the landscape, as now lights vanish bit by bit, like the metronome of New York buildings astorm with blackening after midnight. With each new obliteration comes the intrusion of a furred presence, where something—perhaps a light—once shone out, as if a creature now bustled in space. Was it this new intoxication that led ancient peoples to see in the miles between the stars a trembling stream, darkening and invisibly lit with a new and antique intelligence?

MANHATTAN PSALM

The choiring seas of bodily exultations
Exalted in their depths, their spirit-ministrations,
Sing fish in my veins, sing mammals and plants,
Leap through my lungs in slums, on avenues—
Their mordant green obituary of light,
Their preachment of decay, of blue transformation
Travel in my sea-breath, ocean-sway, nod
With all their providential cellular change.
My syllables oceanic, eyes of newest stained glass
Rise blinking from the glossless ocean depths
Where all things purr and hunt in brainy silence still,
Still—
New optics showing these lit fish in the dark.

Kiss, taste, in the submarine
Green blue of your eyes' frank sea.
God, God, all the rage I free
Blast-kissing your breast in pain.

Change, change into something wet
Heart-storm of the world's old hate,
Soul-skin of your woman's heat
Let rain all the rage I get

Day after foul day like fuel
Stored hard in my place of storm
So now in this bed you warm
We two may turn fine what's cruel.

NUDE WOMAN

A whitened brook at night, as pearly icing
Extravasates on mounds of chocolate
And sends a white confection through a forest.

FINDING HER PHOTOGRAPH

Monsters by twilight and the crazy twitter
Of hunching things.
You come around me as an old equation
Resolving the dark.
Years later, you turn me quadratic
With passionate unknowns—
What if?—what then?—your graphing of a sigh,
Your mathematics on film
Of beasts and aching and vast breathless planets.

AFTERMATH

A slippery sleep. A beached and monstrous eel
Ropes fast across my mind's hushed nightfall dunes
Vestibuling its ocean—the bloodstained waves
That master waves leash in past wakefulness—
The eel's bright skimming head, its quivering crop
A smoky speed.
                        What else could I have said?
Is she awake now too, somewhere, sleep-slipping,
Staring, like me pathetic, at monstrous failure?

LIQUID

The delphic springs of the health-giving sulphurous waters—
Sources—
Where else but here, when else but now, with whom else
But you, whose feminine sulphurous eyes mark all?

COLOR ÉTUDE

Such sovereign light waves liquify the pansy
Of purple pouring violet on magenta,
Oasis of pouring,
The eye camels the brain past metaphor

Till black deep center becomes big-bang dark
Of earliest creation that stretches nets,
Sheer cosmic strings,
Trapping the nomad universe in its tent.

AUTUMN SPECIMENS

In the wind, the trees gibber. On the beach, spectres of mist stagger into the sun, waving amorphous limbs to be amputated by the axes of waves. The sand beneath my feet smells of mountains and grass, of landlocked countries. Shapes reform their skeletons. A hare, bounding over a rut of sand, changes into a giant neolithic hound chasing ghosts. An apple tree becomes a pterodactyl making a kiting stand against extinction. A doe, developing into an ice-age mountainous elk, steps into the gray glow of lava waves blowing out, blowing in from the sea. In the sea, Atlantis descends beneath ashes. A new threat rises to float in my mind, in the air—impossible to distinguish which—a state of cunning like a palace.

STILL LIFE: BANANA

You peel a yellow parabola
Exposing a white parabola
Snaking with sugar, potassium.
On jetty after-midnights
One liveried moon
When left a simple sliver
Reverses all
These peels of light.
The white parabola, crisping,
Yellows as it sinks,
Dresses itself in light waves,
Slips a ballroom sheath of yellow
Straight up mermaid tail and waist,
Across its shimmied body
Till dressed it vanishes,
Parachuting its sleek apparel from the dark.

The Trek to the Far Corners of the Earth

Thickets of staggering people, I push through them,
Whole forests leafy with hands, trunky, branchy,
The old proud ones too, people condensed,
Accretions of glances in their glades,
The snow-white seasons and their harvest falls too,
All seasons of their accelerating muscles,
Their voices like insects, locusts, bees, crickets—
The summer-season voices, inquisitive, shy:
And more trees, birch, oak, maple, even redwood,
Sometimes soft sunny spots between their plantings
Or stormy ones where lightning sweeps hotly—
Staggering blameless thickets, forests of the journey,
Traffic of true nature and the character of gravity.
I exalt the marvelous forests where I wander,
Exalt the subtle peace, the competitions,
I remember the sweat of the path, the feminine slopes,
The masculine blowings—the people wind.

SOMETIMES

Sometimes I know the Age of Dinosaurs
Frets on, it never ended, just diminished,
The armored beasts heaving
Desperately across the landscape
Still, in plusher smaller quixotic bodies,
Like all the Roman gods and goddesses
Who shrank in terror before the Christian God,
Becoming leprechauns, and faeries, elves,
Implausible creatures, haunting the forest glens
Hiding
Pausing
Making their primitive cackling promises
To the unsuspecting traveler tired of life
And all its frank remorseless needs.
The lost beasts bask in the brain
Promising the desperate power of escape,
Extinction
Brainless terror—
I know their monstrous grace
And all dinosaur days
Bring me their dark permissions
In great reptilian stalkings of the skies.

ORPHEUS

His music, as once I heard it near Thrace, his lyre that mimicked
the notes of the spinning planets and lured the celestial hymn
and wild lullaby of stars and galaxies to human ears, the first
ghostly music, the music that purloined the notes of heaven, as
Prometheus, risking his life, stole fire from the gods—and then
his voice that calmed and stirred afresh mountain streams,
tricked oaks into fantastic growth, beat into blithe silk the hard-
est woman's heart—both lyre and voice alone, as one, in the
frisky air of night, made, I could hear it, the same elective effect
as occurs when I walk alone along a city avenue, maybe
Columbus Avenue, jammed and hot in June, full of noise, the
shops open, apace, the traffic buzzing, the people abustle, and
turn into a sidestreet, the notes and gossip hushed, the darkness
brushed and caught between the trees and hanging like a web,
where suddenly, over the patient townhouses, and quiet and
fixed and round there, a spectre of alien skin, a ghost-skin
spreading a space so yellow and lacquered and vast that my eyes
blow out and into it as vision-winds, the moon adduces me,
sucking my words into syncopation.

LETTER FROM AIOLIA

I personally know Circe. She unbraids her symphonious raven hair nightly in her loft in SoHo. Men, turned into senescent swine under her spell, oink at her over the telephone, or on the tape she leaves in her answering machine. Penelope, whom I also know but find myself seldom wanting to visit, lives on the Upper West Side, knitting, staving off suitors, worried about the sturdy son she must nurture alone, because his father disappeared long ago, first into a modern Trojan War fought over conference tables in midtown, then into Circe's loft. At night, too, I meet Tiresias on the Bowery, besotted and full of prophecies—all man, having spent seven years as a lovely woman. Athena alights in various disguises beside him, sometimes as a flashing neon sign, often as a headlamp on a passing Mercedes, one that Tiresias and I examine and swiftly nod over, because its bizarre glint, more chaste than other headlamps, chatty yet military, lets us know that the goddess of skills and skulls flits always about us. The Gorgon sisters mutter over garbage baskets on Central Park South, collecting discarded soda cans for worthless nickels, gigantic in motheaten furs, menacing-faced with their aspish Gorgon hair, so long, wanton as decay. I meet Telemachus on Friday evenings, when he leaves Penelope to visit and stay overnight with me. But we do not discuss the quest for his aging hero-father, the wiliest warrior and most cunning statesman known to the ancient world. Nor do I tell him that long ago I ceased to be that Odysseus, that clear-eyed wanderer, charmed by the lotus-eaters on Columbus Avenue, and am now changed, perhaps by Circe, perhaps by my guardian Athena, into an ordinary man. We discuss our world, our own wine-dark sea of a city-world, in which everything remains possible, and I urge on Telemachus the deep wonder of studying the ancient poems so that he can see about him.

JONAH AWAKENS TO HIS MISSION AS PROPHET

This was a land of scrawny air and sunlight.
The dryness pared his words.
A crow sat editorializing on a branch.
The province drowsed.

He kicked aside a snake. His hot feet hurt
And when he spoke the air creaked like arthritis
Chalked in a thermometer of white sky.
One horsefly bobbled.

His tunic stank of fish. He spoke of rain,
A storm, a plumping wave,
Then darkness that ignited blazing prayer
Inside a beast.

No one looked up. He blinked for languid seconds
And paused, with all the night there in his throat
And nowhere else. This was the land of day
And exiled blood.

He would need nights aswarm with frightened pleasures.
He would need godless nights.
The bestial people—at Nineveh—the crazed ones
Would be all ears.

AFTER THE EMPIRE FELL

> The dogs and vultures at Grand Cairo
> did, on the withdrawal of the Roman
> legions, bring up their young together.
>
> —Hasselquist, *Travels to the Levant*

The dogs and kites of Cairo nursed their young
Snarling and croaking near new pyramids,
Black waste-hills near the pharoahs' pyramids,
With Egypt shrieking under a vulture's tongue.

At Rome the sky became a hard blue lizard
Arching and fixing its godless blurry eye
In golden hatred on the Pantheon.
The bones of Augustus blanched in August heat.

Athenians and far-off Celts dreamed of escape.
In Rome the eye stared at the bewildered millions
Packing up. Young boys dreamed of fat figs
Ripening now in the hot safe countryside.

Whores rutted in the temples. Foreign pigs
Went mad among them. Soldiers hooted. Hope
Coughed among the rats while games of hazard
Made dead men their cold tables. Smart men died.

It would be centuries, they guessed, before the sky
Once more appeared a tender paraclete.
Meantime: the dust and smell and mad cotillions
Of exiles hiding and lunching and lurching on,

Forgetting the bitter quest for sensate order
And spirit-peace. Who knew Rome meant that much?
Or that to heal the world would take as much
As fifteen solid centuries of murder?

CELLINI'S FLIGHT FROM ITALY

(Winter, 1561)

All day they rode among white hills and came at sunset
Among cold winds to a land like permanent high noon,
An earthbound system of sun and planets tossing
Imperially among white mountains high above them.

"Switzerland," said Cellini, touching his Perseus,
The silver dwarf-replica of his giant statue,
Slaughterer of Medusa, exhibited in Florence.
The replica impaled the dwarf-stars of the mountains,
Cellini unwrapping it from its chamois sleeve, dazzling,
And against the white of the hills and spellbinding alps,
The crimson dark that sleeved around him, snakelike,
A defiant laser that gleamed and curved in his fingers,
Sinewy despite the cold, adept and cool in his hands,
Crystal antinomy, a silver egoless ray—
His ticket of escape more brazen than Mont Blanc.

"The King of France," he said with snowy calculation,
Arranging his cloak and bending imperially windward,
"Invites us to the other side of the bitter world,
Just past winter, and should pay."
                                        His pack-boy snorted,
A bold, fat, lippy creature, useful if ignorant,
Extracted from some Florentine alley for his billowy grace,
Some dream of obedience, a cheap boy like a troll and pillow,
Smooth-cheeked, sly, unimpressed by the King of France
Or his master's fame, a boy like the ridiculous public
For art itself, corrupt and purely instinctual,
Cynical and forgetful.
                        Cellini sighed, remembering

The boy's hot fifteen-year-old sister, an anemone
Of sea-dark responses, sea-sweet currents and sweat,
Modeling for his sweet gold statue of Psyche one minute
And shivering in his sheets the next, exultant, prissy,
A girl shivering in wonder. Her father's bill of rape,
A manufactured fang, Cellini thought, a ruse
For blackmail—God, the girl embarrassed art and love!—
What worshipper of gold as light and light as gold

Could possibly refuse those golden sullen lips?—
Had chased him here, the city watchmen bribed, the haste
In packing up a few gold statuettes, the need
To run a corporal through before the fearful gallop
Past Giotto's dazzling tower and Brunelleschi's dome,
Across the Arno, northward, on the run from death,
A hunted rapist now.
                                        The sunset stabbed the snow
And bloodied it a little. Coughing, sleepy, staring
In silence at the mountains reddening, the boy,
Phlegmatic, hungry too, ignored the bloodied snow
That reddened his fat cheeks and horse.
                                        Cellini said,
"God's test," allowing these two words to blow away
And scatter on the wind. "This is, like art, God's test."

At once a vision like another solar system,
A mental one of spiritual white planets,
Displayed him to himself, afloat, careering, sure,
Explorer sailing on, his brazen skiff white fire.
He traveled on a sea of light, a sea of shadows,
Of known and mutant, brilliant, whipping, plasmic, holy,
Whose waves of liquid gold, hot silver, bronze in currents
He ladled into moulds. He felt he tasted metal.
He knew he dipped into the precious mind of God.
He lifted out the silver beam of Perseus.

And watched the spacious eyes of one who worked in stone,
Those eyes of Michelangelo that heaved great hills,
Rough, uncut, of marble, as he inquired
Had you any idea the struggle in making a thing?
The sheer cost of the pain?—eyes heaving stones,
Dark filthy ones that needed chipping, polishing,
Not to mention rotten demands on muscles, brains,
Archaic gems of memory he must recover, chip
Blindly from his past—while sipping his glass of wine—
Rough as marble hills behind his hilly eyes.
A vacant desert stretch of spirit lay past them
Where your eyes overleaped the hills of his and saw
Past uncut hills of stone a frozen storm of sand
Trembling in the heat, yet frozen, still, crisp,
Alive as the deathless castles of chilly heavens.

His vision turned to deliquescence in his mind.
He heard himself exclaiming through the argent air,
Ignoring winter, Switzerland, the orphaned mountains,
As if he had to, scarcely knowing how he did it:

"The planet echoes in its fastened trees and buildings,
Listen, with cries and gasps of death, like old flowers
Pressed into the pages of scrapbooks, deaf human flowers.

Forgotten rages, clashes, alarums haunt the masonry.
The beatings of horses, creakings of catapults, listen,
Still sound in the hills from battles fought long ago.

The desperate planet aches. Its orb encircles pain
And releases pain into our nerves in moments of rash silence.
Just listen. Pain stalks our souls. Just wander any city street,

In any city, and under the distracting traffic you must hear,
Oh, listen, the deathless dying rustle of massacres.
The children, women, the knights pierced with deadly arrows,

Audible if you listen with an observing ear, crying out
And piercing you with anguished words, deep horrid gougings,
The lances that once rifled flesh, the slitting daggers—

All whisper damage done among the indifferent stones.
The damage pierces us. Art makes the only healing, art,
That prayer beyond mere wishing, that soothes the infected spirit.

The cruel songs trapped in the stonework, frightened questions
Tossed on meadowed countrysides too lush with grass,
Grass fattened on spilled blood, present their haunted premise,

That all these victims died to let us walk here.
And art like whispers of the patient universe
Promises us hard indefatigable recognitions.

Even here in the snow, where Hannibal fought southward,
Inviting his brother's head, unwitting, to decapitation,
No spot, though pure and clean and sterilized with cold,

Is innocent. Beneath the opalescent snow,
As in true opals, flickers one thin proverb flame,
A ghostly fire, and a ghostly solemn voice,

The songless voice that sings, the solemn singing bones
Whose ambient song I hear, and cannot, do not, know.
I cannot possibly imagine how it sounds."

The boy said he was hungry. Above them flowed white stars
In blessed sensate streams through heaven's renaissance,
A senate of light laws, democracy of reason,
A politics of brittle common sense lit up,
In which he trusted.
                    Feed the boy. Bed down. Rise early.
It was an adolescent evening of leaps and stops,
Of glare and spurt that riveted the shadows of snow,

The whiteness lurking, as if the sun lay back and huddled
And fastened in itself, the snow unpleating at it,
A bluish whiteness, awkward, immature and slick.

Ahead—but who could know it—lay a sparkling threat.
At sunset two days hence, they would be climbing hard,
A narrow mountain trail. The horses ankle-deep
And slipping, panting, laden with his only statues,
In risky snow. The wind a giant's powerful axe
Chopping out the sun with mad thick chops of snow,
Imperial axe that cleft air close and squalid-white
And loud, the wheezing horses, mountless, dazzled
With fear, the boy a solemn pillow leading them,
And he behind, half blind with frozen latching eyelids—
All sceneless in a vicious alien dispersion
Of mountain-planets, dim.
                              And then the lazy falling.
It would come quietly. At first, as if infections
Of gravity itself caused it to lose its power,
The horses looked as if they ambled up white billows
And mounted heavenwards. The boy sailed up with them,
A marbly whiteness closing. Then, when they were gone,
Sucked into bliss, and he, confused, stood isolated,
In jealous loneliness for seconds, sight came back,
Returning on the wind, in dread, the whiteness winking.

He saw the horses' hoofs, greased black with ice, shoot out
Across the edge of cliff, and grottoes of their mouths,
Dark panic dens, black ambling nostrils, despumating.
The boy slipped blackly, wheeled his arms, and shot askance,
And he too, stiff with terror, felt his footing slither,
His body wrinkling toward the destitute abyss,
A sheer five-hundred feet of blackness masticating.

This would take seconds, and in those seconds rhythms
And visions of his memory would flood his mind.

He would be falling, smelling blood, as that sweet girl
Who modeled for him smiled, as Michelangelo
Said something strange—that marble was more valuable, costly,
Than gold and silver, far more spiritual, outlasting,
When all was said and done, pure human greed, the sort,
When all was said and done, that would lead even kings
To melt down gold and silver statuettes of heroes,
Of gods and goddesses, and even those by him,
The greatest silversmith the world had ever seen,
For money.

        He would feel his wriggling body topple,
The iciness of hopelessness, the fear of hell,
Fresh hell, the blackest maw, the final gristled throat,
Horselike, thoughtless, cold.

                He would—"Oh, God," he cried—
Begin to pray, to beg, with shatterings of wind
And ice and sucking ripping at his throat and mouth
And swallowing his words, his skinny fingers touching.
He dropped, would drop somehow, to both his lizard knees
That swarmed and stuck, like lizard bodies on the wall
Of some adobe house in bitter summer heat,
All thirsty cold—amazed at praying, shocked in fact
By what he said and could not say, in fact not praying
For mercy for himself, no, not for him, his life,
His Perseus, but comprehending then and there
That somehow they would make it past this place and live,
Survive the threat, the snow, survive the miracle,
The miracle of horrid testing. He said, "Oh, God,
I thank you. Help the boy. Help him. I thank you, God,
For bringing me this far, filling my life with wonders,
And for preparing what you must prepare, whatever."
That would be the planet prayer he whispered then.

STILL LIFE: CRUCIFIXION

They shadowboxed the nails. Darkness fell at that
As if the pagan sun, a suicide,
Unlit itself. No one could hear a thing,
And there were many there, except a tearing
From near the top of all three high wood crosses
As if the three men up there wriggling
Masticated valuable manuscripts.

The watchers heard internal blackness crypts
Creak in their throats, acquiring niggling
Suspicions that their speechlessness meant losses
Blacker than the losses they stood sharing
(The loss of sight, the loss of shadowing)
As if perspective, brusquely blown aside
On some vast canvas, left the painting flat.

Their eyes flew upward at the alien sky,
One byzantine square dark in two dimensions.
A soldier lit a torch. Flat light sloped forth,
A ship's hull cracking open, leaking, listing,
And in the dark spilled scarlet on the wood
High overhead and muscles kneading pain
Where fingers, chucking splinters at escape,

Grasped quickly at a vein of larcenous hope
And where their lacerating morbid strain
Culled bloodied centuries. None understood,
Or would, their final quasi-human fisting:
Three brains convulsions with subtracting earth,
Three bodies' casual animal suspensions,
Six eyes brisk whiskings out on one flat sea.

LA SAINTE-CHAPELLE

(modified sestina and right-hand-end-word acrostic)

La Sainte-Chapelle in Paris flees thought and form
And each wall of glass aflame in sunlight blesses
Your deepest human wish to escape your flesh.
Accept the gift. Accept your fact of spirit,
That this antique glassy house of prayer enjoys
Your metamorphosis into purest thought

As if the house assisted purest spirit
And burst through itself like a lover who enjoys
The love so much that flesh bursts into form
And there like fire turned smoke, climbs into thought
And more than thought, an ecstasy that blesses
The slightest movement of his dissolving flesh.

I climb the winding stair without a thought
Of all this power, urbane, one who enjoys
Flesh and bone and thought far more than spirit.
The stair climbs from old mortuaried flesh
Below, of buried kings, through dark that blesses
My simple sense that I possess a form

Already complete, with no earthly need of spirit.
Above, just past the dark, the chapel blesses
(I naïvely feel) believers craving form
And yearning for some sweet ceremony of thought.
But I feel myself complete, a traveler who enjoys
Good architecture as if it were fine flesh.

The simple truth: I know less than my flesh,
Know only my dark, the climbing. So the house enjoys
As if alive, my sheer surprise of spririt

As I reach the topmost stair with the careless thought
That only the climbing matters: a dazzling blesses
And lightens me with light turned solid form.

Great windows peel to heaven. A spirit-form,
The form of biblical light in glass, enjoys
A vast glass-fleshing of the earliest thought
And around me rise the creation of the flesh,
The murder of dark, of guilt, a story that blesses
The triumph of a flesh-escaping spirit.

My very flesh turns numb, flush with the thought
That all is glass that enjoys its bursting form
And that burst of insight blesses me with spirit.

LINES FOR A DRAWING BY BURT HASEN

A blast of black.—The painter Titian said
Masterfully of his great, final black period,
His blasts of it in paint and black fleshy ink,
Boiling clothes of it, jewels trembling in black,
That black sufficed: if your eyes ascended
Powerlessly into it, a crystal formed,
A prism twisted in your unbounded mind,
Dazzling your surrendered eyes with colors.

I get this now. You send me from your loft
In Dutch Street, where your fingers work in shadows,
A black sketch like a blast—a woman turns
And surrenders forever in one perpetual motion
Of ink, ascending in black crystalline clothes,
And giving me the astonished white cloud of her face.

SWINBURNE AND MAUPASSANT AT ÉTRETAT, 1868

"just the facts, please"

The wizened hand was Swinburne's, who lunched on monkeys,
Then Maupassant's, who bought it, fascinated,
At some point (though no one remembers the exact day)
After seeing it at the poet's house in Étretat.
There Maupassant had been invited at about noon
After saving the little fellow, then just thirty one
But already the author of his *Poems and Ballads* and *Calydon*
And famous, with his outsized head,
From drowning while he was swimming in the Channel.

A crowd had gathered. The many who watched his splashing,
Astonished, recalled the exasperating summer heat,
And Swinburne himself gone limp amid the currents
And Maupassant, just eighteen, but swimming well
And undismayed by the spinneys of secret water forces,
Catching and pulling, then both staggering up the beach
Breathless, and afterwards the poet's public invitation
To come to lunch: "Please join me. I seem to be having monkey."

Quite clean and cool and crisp, the future novelist obliged—
And then was shown that heavy wizened hand, shellacked,
That Swinburne fancied as a paperweight.

This item later appeared in a tale of Somerset Maugham's.
You surmise that even earlier the hand was Poe's
Though one cannot know for certain.

In this sharp way do special hooks and nets
Intrude upon the calm of literature—
A swimming incident, a lunch
And a loose end, so to speak,
An unidentified but salvaged human hand

Displayed across a famous poet's desk.

                    Oh, and the cooked-up monkey.

From such facts, too, one can deduce the weather,
Conceding with those who witnessed Swinburne's rescue
That sun and heat that day were of a special hardness.

Auras and Haloes

An investigation of images

A man orders coffee. Under his breath, he mutters, "C'est la loi," over and over. I recognize the phrase as a gambler's silly expression, as coming from Baudelaire's poem "Le Jeu," about the addiction of gambling, its horror like mould gathering prematurely on the body of a dying invalid, and wonder whether the man has read the poem. He looks fierce enough, small and compact enough, here in this coffee shop in Greenville, North Carolina, where I've stopped off for an hour, to be literate, but you never know. He may never have heard of Baudelaire.

He seems to have no eyes. He bends over the plastic table top. His cheeks are unshaven. He wears a lumberjack's red-checked shirt. He looks filmy with sweat and filth, not farmer's filth but the sort that develops on the clothes and skin of someone who does not care and does not bathe, enlarging him a little, like a grainy photograph in which details such as hands become icons. His hands, I notice, are reddish brown. They twitch as he picks up his coffee.

Two boys come in and stare at him.

He mutters, "C'est la loi."

A prawn embedded in a cube of plastic rests on the table beside him.

Images reticulate light. Money pouches have gone out of style, soon money. A jingling passes from the atomosphere. The reticulations of the law, once icons, are now images whose secrets, incomprehensible as the reason for light and vanished wealth, whisper through the mouths of imagined moments.

In the heads of the Amazon indians, as they prepared to chop down teak for longboats, and afterwards, amid the felling and joy, the burning and happiness, the fires beside the river in the night, the dances, the conversations, the long fires banked the lengths of the tree trunks, always as they watched and waited for the moment when the wood grew pulpy with ashes for the hollowing, swam visions of a fleet, vast ranks of military transports that formed up, first by twos, then hundreds, abreast on the river of galactic power, of liquid atomic restraint, deep with beasts under its waves, while on its banks patrolled human and inhuman beings waiting for slavery, conjuring the navy of longboats, of trunks newly hollowed and laden with warriors, costumed ploughmen of ashes, painted igniters of the stars, men grown into power and joyful wounds, brawls, conversations about blood and slaughter, igneous-minded beside their floating murderous knives.

At the public fountain on the rue de la Roquette, in the Eleventh arrondissement, a man, his mind in flames, chatters about long-boats and water. At noon, in the sun, he speaks in "l'argot de l'armée de Napoléon" about felled trees, battles, and a dance he calls "J'avais la puissance de l'eau" to a woman coming from a flower shop with epiphitic orchids.

We—she and I—live in the aftermath of icons, the aftermath of symbols. It is of greater importance, I am coming to believe, living among senseless relics, to understand the augury of this. This is the pre-religious era, before Neolithic caves, the pre-symbolic era, before Iron-Age scratchings in sand, in stone, on bark, of human signs. Yet we two inhabit a dwelling managed by artificial intelligence. We read newspapers, look at paintings. We talk with friends, pay bills, taxes. It is hard to understand right away, amid these operations, that even our most innocent glances, the smallest objects, slightest gestures, least utterances, perhaps even this that I am writing, are relics of symbols: that icons vanished one hundred years ago, and that since then symbols have disappeared. To put this differently, perhaps more comprehensibly: we know that war is no longer war, peace no longer peace, friendship no longer friendship, love no longer love. Human society in the old sense no longer exists. Neither do governments, rulers. Words themselves change before our eyes and vanish. Old quests vanish. We know that this is as true of science as of art. In art, permanence equalled truth. In both art and science, equations meant beauty. The quest for the permanence of beauty no longer exists, except among residual cults, minute groups that will soon disappear, and religious fanatics seeking a reversal of history at the cost of slavery, whose contempt for life is perfect.

Images remain.

To purchase the reddest rose you need a lot of luck. Before trying, before visiting flower shops or hunting for the reddest rose out of town, it is worthwhile watching a spider, not a real spider but a spider in memory.

Then purchase the reddest rose. Trouble free.

The spider has no flesh. No spider has flesh. It has no feet, hands, knees, hair, nose, ears beyond a seismographic sympathy with atmospheric reticulations in the gaseous vicinity proximate to its body, no arms, shoulders, business. The spider has no web. When the spider contracts, it has the dimensions of a zero, an idea, or a bud, also an idea, or that its spider secret is that it is not an idea but an image, an image that is a series of successive and pensioned nos.

She, the woman I live with, has no spidery qualities. Now you know her.

The magnificence of not minding is most important to an investigation of images, especially not minding about meanings. It is of crucial importance, for instance, not to mind how long it may take for her voice to burst in here, into the investigation. It is important not to think of this possible occasion as a game, even though we are playing it, to comprehend that minding about meanings, like the issue of caring when she speaks, is now obsolete, a relic of a dramatic age. Drama no longer exists. Curiosity about it disturbs nothing, is itself an obsolete instrument that creates no reticulations. If she speaks, she will do so in her own good time, in tones inaudible on this page and with resonances kept secret from sound.

To sit alone in an igloo when the wind is down is to wait in a potential drum. Outside are no trees, no spiders, no sounds, and only the secret. The Aleutian eskimos, while cutting with bones the silent cubes of snow and ice for their structures, while manipulating the cold blocks between their mittens, feeling the warmth and thickness of their fur clothes, glad and anxious, hands deft in the essential silence of air and leagues of snow before the drumming wind came, formed always in their minds a village of igloos, of silent round structures resisting the single heavenly beat, of winter music with only one stroke that would come when it came with fierceness and perfection, freezing every liquid for miles around, preventing every movement but its own, and they raced in their minds toward their silent vision of a village of igloos repaired from the wind, with the liquids of their bodies beating, humbled, beating.

Images lack psychology. This is not true of symbols, and certainly not true of icons, which also possess spiritual content. There is a purity of images, and a purity of collections of images, lifting them in the mind and memory out of the corruption of motives, drives, obsessions and needs, which may not exist. Images do not grow or develop. They simply exist, and the existence of each one always seems a miracle, like Venus exiting full blown and perfectly beautiful at birth from the sea. Conscience and even ethics play no role in the process of the creation of images. Conscience is often appalled and at least frightened by the process, because it implies frivolity, indifference to established perceptions, and rebellion, though the truth is the opposite: any image must be part of the purity, an expression of Law. Images need not be beautiful to be beauty and to sanctify Law, as plastic may enclose a prawn, reflect a man's face, indemnify a moment.

Once it was possible to speak about the past as if it was over. Now it is possible to do so only with respect to the present, as if it were eluctibly here: the prawn, the floating knife, the block of snow, the first emotion.

THE THEORY OF SOARING

I tell you there is nothing more beautiful, among the many beauties of the human form, than the skeleton. I think of the lovely ribs, polished by translucent glowing lymph, of the women I meet in restaurants, their silver spines tooling beneath their tan or white skins, the somber bones of their fingers as their hands trace routes through the light, the mobiles of the bones of their knees, canvassing, pressing, as they cross their legs, the caressing weight of their thigh bones at luxuriant rest in their bodies' ponds—and the feather-blades of their shoulders, like wings rising and rippling beneath their skin-prisons, and glimpse flights, always flights, held back but waiting to soar, in their living wild skeletons, flights restrained by the flesh of sweet and seamless patience.

RENDEZVOUS

She brings me her skull behind her angry smile. Her skull, I see, is not angry—salubrious bone, calm, philosophical. I take her skull to lunch, later to bed, waiting for the smile to pass in the earthy exhaustion of all rage, feeling the droll beauty of her skull, its perpetual rest, now, in my palm, its wit.

MY ANTIQUE FRENCH CLOCK

He sits like a plump old man, a dwarf in a club-room chair, gossiping about lost youth while convinced he is talking about a spanking-clean future. "Tomorrow . . . next year . . . in ten years," etcetera. The round pale face glows with tipsiness. He tries to camouflage his disorientation with monotones. People passing by listen by accident. Yet the umbrageousness of his voice is essential as a secret wallet. I require this gossiping plump man, villatic, who sustains in his tunnels of minutes a last belief in fruits and health, in lemon-scented palaces, in meadows where chrysanthemums flare and fade, in visions of blue lagoons, in a woman's hand slipping hotly over flesh.

THE SCROLLWORK ASPECTS

The lacquered red screen of her mouth, as if
As if she dresses and undresses, if
As she spins there in her Chinese dark, as
If it mattered ever so slightly, stands
Red and perfect as if before my mouth.

Or she transgresses through blue opium smoke
Screwing her body out of it, smoke
Blue-screwing through my eyes, the opium
Smoke there, screwing out, as she smokes
Rich and smoky white out of her blue mask.

THE TRAINING Á LA DIOGENES

I sought the buccaneers of nutrient visions,
The crisp architects of spaces beyond structures,
Within structures—the warm enthusiastic doubters,
The lovers without appointments, outlawed law-givers
Forever truculent among oafish legislators of goods—
I sought orchid makers, epiphitic gardeners of spirit

The hunters not of land but of landscape, their eyes' caress
Of optical terrains of mind planning settlements of spirit
In lakes, on peaks, in valleys of imperial shadow,
In imperial sunlit light adumbrious with reason,
Their eyes triangulating new ghostly locations
By animal geometries of sea and sky.

MOVING PICTURE

The ship sneaked under the storm. For seconds both
Turned wary beasts of prey, the smaller scrambling
With cutting viciousness, the latter spectral,
Pawing. Yellow light stalked fast between them,
A sleek celestial tiger. The ship hunched low
And slunk and nipped about. The light described
Its fangs across the upper deck and worried
Straight through the windows on the saucy bridge
Behind which three pale figures could be seen
And hands gesticulating. The light leaped high
At rolling equant clouds, its fang-holes letting
Thick fonts of water loose like monstrous blood.

A bittern hung amazed in the rude air,
Blew into ragged sails, fell to the deck,
Washed overboard.
                          You could have dropped a pin:
The silence of the galaxies was perfect.

HOW THE WORLD BEGAN

and this is how the world ends,
Not with a bang but a whimper.
                                    —T.S. Eliot

It started with a bang, however it ends—
A single proton word, neutronic syllable,
A piston-whisper at the birth of light
Sexing the birth of time
From zero
A zero packaged
As crammed laws
Bright zero
The blossom of nothing—
The startled big-bang word
Banging round
And heaving from chest to mouth in the chestless dark.

You know there was a telescope ear that listened,
Heard echo the sexing syllable of brightness
A dark-bright skinless ear that shivered
At the sex of time
Of light
The gender time of light
And that it listens
Now
Attending us
As we two package
Through penetration
That earliest sigh-gasp
Whispering light from zero in ghostless nanoseconds:

Astronomers hunt its eluctible pale traces—
The ghostly biblical glen of the blazing word
Peering toward that gravity ghost-garden

Out there
Far out
Where close to zero
Shivers
And listens
To soundings
The telescope
Like a microphone
Lowered
Beside a lost steep whale
Diving into her sex cry in the Pacific.

We live among those blossoming echoes, hunting
The decibels in you and me and hearing
Them, our human ears like whales trembling
Against your ache
Your syllable
Your word
As you come
Aching,
Your telescoping body
Unpackaging the birth-time
With its ache
And firing it at the divinity of the dark.

THE BLAZING AGE

Now comes the blazing age of war and love,
Never the rudeness sharper, more inspired,
More hectic for detonation—
The science and freedom equally perfected
So that the rumored atomic apocalypse
Accompanies your bravest sweetest kisses.

Extremes in fierceness perpare the planet for blazing,
The universal worship of heat gone mad
With mental atomic winds
And sex winds blazing—and whether of war or love
Or some princely atomic accident
Only the beast knows that lashes the human soul.

THE FLAME CHARTS

It is the mapless energy of grace
I wish to map, seeking loose frontiers
Where lovers tangle flamelike
As the curtsy of two flames
Flares, nods
Nods back in hot oxygen politeness,
The bright exalting zone.

STILL LIFE: THE GARDEN OF PTOLEMY

You sense the inertia, or it senses you, as an aroma, not as powerful as that streaming from a pyramid of roses, not as pungent with nostalgia as that rising from the memorized breasts of a woman friend after love, neither earthy, nor light, nor acrid as a geranium leaf torn from its ample dark stem, but plump and recollective as peace among wet boughs in September. The aroma strews its ancient garden in you. The garden is a sweet jurisdiction of surrender. You recognize the old intimacy and wonder where you have been, discollecting yourself, trafficking among ruins.

All sense of personal plot vanishes. The garden, with its intimacy, becomes all universe. What else can universe be, in your depths as well as on your surface, but a smoothing between wrinkles of opposites? What else, after the first black explosion? What else can death be but the predictable stilling of bewilderments? Equivalences equal the soul. Long, long before you are aware of the colors here, the sounds, the textures, you feel yourself stray among familiar equivalences: a plume of Greek columns like that of the most ancient temple of Aphrodite, with the perfume, so lax and implicit, of marble that has aged very well. Your skeleton pauses.

A bell tolls. It tolls once. Someone walks toward you along a path. In the distance, he appears white-robed, a penciled-in sketch of a piano key without sound. He arranges the lawn's green around him as he walks, wrinkling it into logic. He trusts the confluvium, the garment-lawn that he gathers about him, in the air, in the light, in his movement among astral equations.

CALADIUM

The leaves, flat violet hearts.
The veins, naked.
The veins, resting.
Outside the hermetic heart-skin.
It glides through two dimensions,
Absent thickness,
Invisible in time,
Ticking on its aortal stem,
Instructing vegetable angels.

THE UNIVERSE OF STREETS

I take the cities voluble and freighted,
With beast-lovers hunting through them, whole avenues of lovers,
Those rushed with compensations, posing, shying,
Some demented with imaginary pastures, mental flowers
Rescuing their brains with earth perfumes, sugaring them
With daffodils, asters, luteous lilies, orchids—
The spicing smells of their dream-spirit gardens—
And walk beside their ample fancy gaits, their devious figures,
Grooming the avenue-tiger in my blood, presuming, appalling,
Prowling months through shadowy digressive slums,
Teaching risk and care for old needed spirit flowers,
Hunting Homer and his sea-quest in torn magazines,
Those wind-blown through bald streets—and rage at rage,
Turn ecstatic with sympathy, virile with night,
Hunting coded acknowledgements in pastoral smiles,
In democratic smiles and aristocratic shrugs,
Ghostly among the poor in populist bitter winter,
Those looping at pavement-fires on East Second Street,
Those bending in quadratic heaps at the Manhattan Bridge,
Those asleep on alcoholic sofas of newspapers in parks—
The shivering universe asleep, all of it,
Bending among its galaxies and stooping over newspapers—
And cry your cry, your oh, your finite oh.

RUSHES AND GRAFTS

You rush in with your eyes, as she with hers, as she plants you in her downwind. You root in with your toes, your fingers. Your arms clip, your legs clip, your body insubstantial roots, your hair atmospheric roots, your nose and mouth roots, your ears assumptive roots, your anus earthrooting, your torso a sparrowing root: as a tree is roots, branches rooting and sparrowing: mammal root, democracy of plungings.

SEASIDE

(Beside the docks at six o'clock near Montauk on the Atlantic)

Made more tender by mist, the massy eye
    For which we have no name
Looks coastward, humbling all its telltale light
Among the yellowed silhouettes of boats.
The nuclear glance, hot, impregnable
Across the empty million leagues of space
Docks tendernesses here among the masts,
Furled sails, nets, hulls, the golden tackle
Of the exhausted fishermen of the earth.

They come back daily, before the telling stars
    Come out, and move in the yellow
With sailors' rosary beads, their sweat, spangling their shoulders,
Stalking, shouting, mostly tavernwards,
Their tan flaming muscles bristling
Like the same flame of the eye that makes them shine
Or staying behind, weighing their scaly cargo
In blond light, scalpeling the flounders,
Skinning, filleting, boxing the fish in ice—

Till all of them are here, gathered under the eye—
    The men of smuggled pain
Slicing and skinning the fish in catchy light,
The nutrition light of immaculate ease.
Behind them trail the yellow-shining wavelets
Like the flung-down chips of a godly sawmill
Fleeting it backwards at the massy yellow eye,
Its wooden yellow photon tenderness.
And I go furnished with light-fleets in my soul,

In soul and brains light-keels, light-sails, light-prows,
    Sea-hunting light-fleets,
And take to sea each night as they come in,
These fishermen of the chippy wavelets and fleet muscles,
And take my own fleet out, the wooden hulls hauled
From the sun, Homeric, arguing the quest,
Ablaze with egoless descents, enraptured currents,
Magnetic poles of hunger hauling knowledge
Into splashes of restoried imagination

Where freedom blows in the heat, juice, blast, sperm,
    The current thighs of ocean.
I sail with old invisible sailors, those
Unfashionable passionate ones, lean ghosts
Of grace and freedom, the besieging ones
Charging like horses across a battlefield
Where the dead rise up like waves, peering through their hair,
Its tangled white mass, the horses galloping
Adventures through their historic bodies, sighing,

Collapsing into death again with the billowy
    Aggressive fevers of martyrs,
And sail the old and futuristic tales
Of loss and pomp in adamantine tides,
The waves whose hoar-hair, whitening with the moon,
Belch old Poseidon forth in dead men's grasps,
Fingers clutching the sea god's beard and shaking,
Shaking, shaking, asking the imperious god
For all his power, oh now, oh after centuries.

INTO

Diving into the strange animal,
Diving into the animal-spiritual,
My words as force fields diving me,
I write for the silent ghosts in living lovers,
Those hooting their imperial triumph in the dark—
Plunging into the boil of mutancy, the jewel of stillness,
The sharking breath of evil, even that,
I sing and snuggle voluminous volcanic tress,
Trioecious in its burning potency—
Diving into the hearts of burning and coming up
Explosive as a buoyant swimmer, pearling,

Tossing the white foam at slippery incandescence.

Paul Oppenheimer is a novelist, journalist, translator and widely published short story writer as well as the author of two previous volumes of poetry. He teaches at The City College and The Graduate Center of the City University of New York.

S P U Y T E N   D U Y V I L

Day Book of a Virtual Poet   Robert Creeley
The Desire Notebooks   John High
Answerable to None   Edward Foster
The Angelus Bell   Edward Foster
Track   Norman Finkelstein
A Flicker at the Edge of Things   Leonard Schwartz
The Long & Short of It   Stephen Ellis
Stubborn Grew   Henry Gould
Mouth of Shadows   Charles Borkhuis
Identity   Basil King
The Poet   Basil King
Warp Spasm   Basil King
The Runaway Woods   Stephen Sartarelli
The Open Vault   Stephen Sartarelli
Little Tales of Family & War   Martha King
Cunning   Laura Moriarty
The Corybantes   Tod Thilleman
Black Lace   Barbara Henning
Detective Sentences   Barbara Henning
Are Not Our Lowing Heifers Sleeker Than Night-Swollen Mushrooms? Nada Gordon
Gentlemen in Turbans, Ladies in Cauls   John Gallaher
Spin Cycle   Chris Stroffolino
Kaleidoscope   Joanna Gunderson
Watchfulness   Peter O'Leary
The Jazzer & The Loitering Lady   Gordon Osing
6/2/95   Donald Breckenridge
Ted's Favorite Skirt   Lewis Warsh
ARC: Cleavage of Ghosts   Noam Mor
Don't Kill Anyone, I Love You   Gojmir Polajnar
The Fairy Flag & Other Stories   Jim Savio
In It What's in It   David Baratier
Transitory   Jane Augustine
Psychological Corporations   Garrett Kalleberg